LUMBERJACK

Paintings and Story by William Kurelek

HOUGHTON MIFFLIN COMPANY BOSTON / 1974

For my brother John

Library of Congress Cataloging in Publication Data

Kurelek, William, 1927–
    Lumberjack.

    SUMMARY: The author's paintings of Canadian lumber
camps accompany his first-hand observations of the
life of a lumberjack.
    1. Lumbering — Canada — Juvenile literature.
2. Lumbermen — Canada — Juvenile literature. 3. Lumber
camps — Canada — Juvenile literature. 4. Kurelek,
William, 1927–   — Juvenile literature. [1. Lumber
and lumbering — Canada. 2. Lumber camps. 3. Canada —
Industries] I. Title.
SD538.3.C2K87 1974   634.9'82   74-9377
ISBN 0-395-19922-0

LUMBERJACK is published simultaneously in
the United States by Houghton Mifflin Company of Boston
and in Canada by Tundra Books of Montreal

FOREWORD

Men have gone into the bush for many reasons. The first time I went was in the summer of 1946. I did it to prove to my father (and myself) that I could make it on my own. Like many immigrants, my father had worked in the bush when he first came to this country. And like many fathers, he did not believe that a son could take the hardships he had endured.

I felt I had to go when I did. I was nineteen, in my second year at college, yet I had hardly ever been away from home. Physically, I could do a man's work for, after all, I had been raised on a family farm. But emotionally I felt very immature and dependent on my parents. So when students were being recruited on the campus for a summer job in a lumber camp in northern Ontario, I signed up.

My father was furious. He described the dangers and difficulties of bush life he had known in the twenties and thirties and predicted all kinds of disasters. Trees would fall on me. Bears would attack me. Mosquitoes would eat me. He insisted I was not to go.

His anger lasted until the very morning I was to leave. The day dawned overcast and chilly, to match the depression and guilt I felt about going against his wishes. Then, suddenly, he seemed to relent — I could sense the *snap* even as it happened. He held $20.00 out to me and asked if I would like to have some of his work clothes to take with me.

I guessed the money was just so I would have return train fare when I found it too tough and wanted to come home.

That, he reassured my mother, would be in a week's time. But I stayed the full summer. It was in 1946, and the camp was above Neys, Ontario, directly north of Lake Superior.

When I returned to the bush in 1951, I worked nearly a year, first for a month in a French-Canadian camp near La Tuque on the northern Quebec route of the Canadian National Railway, then at a camp near Fraserdale, Ontario, south of James Bay.

In the past two decades, work in the bush has changed more than it had in the preceding two centuries. It is surprising how little has been written about that remarkable life, and it seems to have been illustrated even less. To re-create it, I have had to depend on my memory — fortunately vivid — and on the few sketches I made then, as well as old photos I sent home. As a painter, I feel very lucky to have experienced traditional lumbercamp living before it disappeared forever.

In some respects all of the camps were as alike as the wood we cut — mostly spruce as pulpwood for the newsprint industry of Canada and the United States. But in other ways, the camps varied according to the national backgrounds of the men who worked in them.

At Neys, Ontario, we were several hundred students working under foremen who were usually of Slavic background (Ukrainian, Lithuanian and Polish). Toward the very end of the summer, when only two other students and myself remained, I worked in a camp with Japanese Canadians from

British Columbia who had been stripped of all their
possessions and interned during the war. The most unusual
thing about their camp was that they had their families
with them. The Quebec camp was uniformly French-Canadian
and French-speaking, with the exception of myself and
four newly arrived Germans. At Fraserdale the majority of the
lumberjacks were Estonian, with a sprinkling of other
nationalities: Finns, Poles, Germans, Ukrainians. The paintings
of the skinny dip after a sauna and the drinking of *kalijaa*
are unique memories from this camp.

Certain bush rules were common to all camps. Two were
"no liquor" and "no women" — although I recall
that one cook was actually a woman married to an Estonian
lumberjack, and at the Japanese camp whole families
were together. I was shy and timid, but from the first I found
myself drawn into the hearty camaraderie that prevailed.
At all camps there was the same yarn-telling, backslapping
humor and feast-sized meals, the same admiration
for physical prowess, skill and productivity.

The combination of exercise, food and fresh air developed
some marvelous physiques. These would be tested
from time to time with the handclasp competition of two
men facing each other over a table or on the floor.
The few students who could match the regular lumberjacks in
tests of strength were understandably proud of themselves.
I remember one episode in particular. George, a Ukrainian
subforeman, was a robust, red-faced man with a
thin neck. One day, seeing some students struggling to move
the corner of a corduroy bridge they were repairing,
he simply bent down over the main beam of the bridge and
with his big hands hoisted the whole structure out of
work's way. There were a few "wows" of admiration. But

Andy, a veterinary student, wasn't to be outdone.
A little while later, when the footing was ready for the main
beam again, he picked up the bridge himself and
returned it to place.

Apart from the log driving, road mending and camp cleaning,
we had to face the hard bush reality of lumberjack
life. We were put on piecework, earning $4.50 for each cord
actually cut and piled. Each of us picked up his
basic lumberman's tools — the swede saw (or Swedish saw, as
it is often called) and the axe — at the company store
and charged them against our earnings. The more delicate
fellows gave cutting a one-day try and then either
asked for work as cook's helper or took the next caterpillar
tractor (or "cat") back to the railway station.

In the evenings Pete and George would listen, a half-smile
playing on their faces, to our bush miseries: stories of
clouds of mosquitoes and black flies; of tripping from fatigue
over twigs and fallen trees; of cords falling apart,
and of blades and handles snapping; of limbs nicked by saw and
axe cuts; of heavy perspiration followed by thirsts so fierce
that even the little pools of soapy water in the muskeg
looked tempting.

For more than fifty years in the forests of Scandinavia, Russia
and North America, the swede saw and the axe had
been the basic tools. I witnessed one of the first attempts to
get rid of them. A few students arrived, armed with
new gadgets called "power chain saws." Flamboyantly, they
gave a demonstration behind the bunkhouse to us
lowly swede-sawyers of how the chain ripped through a fallen
log like a piece of butter. They couldn't wait to get
on their strips to start taking in the money. Pete and George

were skeptical, and their skepticism turned out to be justified. The new machines were so recent that they had not been perfected to run trouble-free.

For a week or so, we swede-sawmen saw columns of blue smoke rising out of the forest where the get-rich-quick guys were at it; and we heard the terrific racket that scared all the forest creatures away. (I eventually worked with a chain saw myself, years later, on my father's farm. The din and vibration were such that even after it was shut off, even after I was in bed trying to sleep, the racket seemed to go right on inside my skull.) Anyway, those early chain-sawyers ran into so many snags, they soon gave up in disgust, packed up their machines and returned to the city. A few lucky ones, like myself, inherited their partly chewed up work strips and partially filled log piles.

I never did get to look like a lumberjack. I was too frail for that. But I nevertheless had a reputation as a worker. My father had been hard on his children back on the land. But he had set us all a good example with his own industry, and he had also taught us to save and stretch money. The result was I didn't dress like a lumberjack, either. I didn't buy one stitch of clothing from the camp store that I could do without. I remember one day George came by on strip inspection and watched me sweating in my ragged red sweater. I told him I wore it because mosquitoes couldn't bite through it, but the real reason was I didn't want to spend money on a proper woodsman's shirt.

The money I earned would, of course, pay for my coming year at university. But what I felt I was really working for all that summer was my independence, my manhood. I didn't even admit to myself that I was homesick; to do

so would have been like admitting defeat to my father. But every time we moved camp, and another group of students used the opportunity as an excuse to return home, nostalgia would grip me. Oddly enough, it was not for the farm, but for those magical first days and weeks in the bush. I shall never forget them: the wraiths of mist rising from our lily-padded lake in the morning; the laugh of the loon echoing over the water in the moonlight; rainy days when the hillsides covered with dark green forest stretched up into the clouds. Sometimes, lying awake at night, I imagined I could hear far, far off the whistle of a train echoing in the valleys. I would follow it in my thoughts all the way down to the driftwood-strewn shores of Lake Superior and on toward . . . I stopped myself, and tried very hard to sleep.

I didn't leave the camp until I passed the 108-workday minimum, the point at which the timber company refunded train fare, both ways. I returned home in time to help with the harvest, and I was welcomed with smiles from everyone, Father included. Wearing my lumberjack boots, I threw myself with a bushman's energy into the farm work: pitching sheaves into the thresher, plowing, hauling grain to the elevator at Stonewall. Outside and inside, I stomped around in those boots, noisily reminding everyone they had been wrong about me, that I had made it on my own.

The second time I went into the bush was five years later, and this time my reason for going was to earn enough to spend several years in Europe studying art. Again, it was in opposition to my father. He had forgiven my first rebellion; after all, I did return to school. But when an immigrant's son was lucky enough to graduate from university, he entered a respectable profession like medicine or law or teaching. I opted for art studies and that was unforgivable.

Eighteen years would pass before he made his peace with me, and I, in turn, realized my boot stomping and grudge bearing had been wrong.

Back then in 1951, I was determined to go to Europe and it looked hopeless when I calculated how long it would take me at most jobs to save enough money. There was only one way I could think of that would get me to Europe faster: going back to the bush as a lumberjack. I was in Montreal at that time, so the employment office sent me to a bush camp in northern Quebec. I arrived in early spring, worked there a month, then went to an Ontario camp where I remained for the rest of the year and well into the winter — until I had the money I needed.

I wish I could write more about that French-Canadian camp but at the time I didn't even speak school French, let alone the *joual* the men used. I stayed only a month and it was rough. I thought I had met some tough lumberjacks in my first camp experience, but nothing, absolutely nothing, prepared me for this experience. Somewhere I had seen a caricature of a *bûcheron* shaving with an axe; it seemed quite possible to me but it must have been drawn on a Sunday because they didn't shave any other day. No one seemed to undress, let alone wash. They wore their clothes until they rotted off their backs, then bought new ones. At the table each made his own tea simply by throwing a handful of leaves into a tin bowl of hot water and drinking from that. The men were making do as best they could, for camp conditions were fantastically primitive. A few years later, I'm told, the unions obliged every camp to have adequate shower facilities and decent quarters for the men.

I was almost completely isolated socially. Only one other person in the camp spoke English. He was a German who had been captured during World War II, sent to a POW camp in the Canadian bush, discovered he loved it and returned after the war to live and work there.

On my arrival at the Quebec camp the foreman gave me a quick once-over and I recognized the expression on his face. It meant: "Nobody who looks like this will ever make it." He decided to speed up the end. The first work strip he assigned me to was on the side of a hill. It wasn't the worst physical ordeal of my life but nearly so. I was out of condition after eight months as a student. The logs had to be 8 feet long, and a few of the trees were 24 inches in diameter at the ground. Even though there were still traces of snow around, mosquitoes and black flies came out in swarms. They crawled into the eyes, mouth and ears, and down the back of the neck. As the month wore on, sandflies joined them. All of them feasted on me. The sweat poured off and my body ached in every muscle and joint. I was half-asleep much of the time as I struggled with those fat logs, pushing them up that hillside on my hands and knees. But I stuck at it. I would make that stake and get to Europe. I would prove I could win — to my father, to myself and to the French Canadians.

And I did. In four weeks I finally finished the hillside strip, but that's when I decided it would be more sensible to cut 4-footers in Ontario and get a bit of social life as well. Just before I left, three other ex-German soldiers came to work in the camp. They talked long hours in my bunkhouse, exchanging stories of war adventures. Once as I looked down from my top bunk onto the gasoline drum-box stove and beyond to the little circle of storytellers thrown into chiaroscuro by the kerosene lamp suspended from the ceiling, I saw a painting. On my way from La Tuque to Ontario I was stuck for two days in the railroad town of Senneterre. I did the painting in gouache, using the paints I had in my knapsack. It was the only painting I actually completed during all my time in the bush.

After crossing the Quebec-Ontario border, I had to spend a night in Cochrane before catching the train to Moosonee on James Bay. To save the cost of a hotel I sneaked into a horse barn and bedded down in the hay.

At Fraserdale, where the lumber mill was located, I was met by a tall, round-faced Estonian in a checkered lumberman's coat. I never did catch his name, though he was to be my fore-man for the next seven months. He and I and two other Estonians walked half a day before we reached the camp — two log barns and a string of tarpapered shacks overlooking a small lake. Here I lived the rest of my lumberjack days — the remaining months of spring, all summer, fall and well into the winter. Except for two weeks during which all the men were dragooned into clearing a tractor road before freeze-up, all I did was cut.

Now to return to the beginning of my story. That day back in 1946 when I first left for the bush, I remember I had trouble finding the train. I had not been on one since I was seven when the family had moved from Alberta to Manitoba. Finally after a long, emotionally trying day, I found the train and boarded it just at sunset. I fully expected to fall into an even deeper depression but immediately, to my surprise, my own sun came up. I felt suddenly exhilarated. Someone began playing a guitar — "There's a new moon o'er my left shoulder, and an old love in my heart" — and a few joined in to sing. It seemed as if everyone on the train was going somewhere great.

1. Arrival in Camp

After hours on the train, five of us got off at the whistle stop
of Neys, and my sense of a great new adventure deepened.
The vastness of Lake Superior was breathtaking to a prairie boy
like myself. The forest behind us stood tall, lush and bold
on the round-shouldered mountains that seemed to march up-
ward and backward from the water's edge. I had never seen
a mountain before in my life.

We took a brief truck ride, which lasted only a few miles, and
then we transferred our baggage and piled the camp
supplies of food and fuel onto a sled pulled by a caterpillar
tractor. The sight of a sled being pulled over bare ground
looked ridiculous to me. But the only other way of transporting
big weights through that difficult terrain was by packhorse
or river boat. The sled was very slow going, but it was sure. We
would jump off it from time to time and walk ahead.
However, water on the road often reached over our boot tops and
forced us back.

I can still hear the clackety-clank-clack-clack of the cat going
over that corduroy road. It was called "corduroy" because
the logs were laid transversely over the watery spots. They were
held together by poles and anchored by stakes at either end.
There were corduroy bridges, too.

One of my first jobs was to work for a week as a helper to one
of the tractor drivers. His nickname was Junior and he
never spoke. He just drove and smiled. Whenever we came to a
corduroy bridge spanning a rocky gorge, I would get off.
To lessen the load on the bridge, Junior first inched the cat
over by itself, playing out the cable off the winch on the
back of the tractor so that the sled remained on the bank.
I would watch him with my heart in my mouth. Would
the bridge hold?

When at last he was safely over, he'd inch the load slowly after
him. That way, if the bridge collapsed, only the tractor
(with him on it) or the sled would be lost.

2. Cook Shack with Bears

A really good cook was the prize boast of any camp and he was
treated with respect because it was so hard to get another
one. This meant he was absolute boss in his area of the camp.
His helpers were called cookees.

Part of the cook's area was the meat shack where whole sides of
cured beef and pork were hung up. The door had to be well
fastened against bears who rummaged in the garbage heap a few
yards off. When the bears weren't there, flocks of ravens
and screaming gulls who had come up from Lake Superior made
it a party place. So much of our food came in cans (pie
filling and lard in pail-sized ones) that the garbage pile sometimes seemed made up of nothing else.

Another important man in any camp was the camp clerk. He
kept track of the number of cords each lumberjack cut and
paid the men. He also ordered the fuel, food and other supplies
and operated the camp store and post office.

3. Lumberjack's Breakfast

The lumberjack's day began when a cookee sounded the camp
gong. This consisted of using a bar of iron to hit a piece
of railway track that had been suspended on a wire near the
cook shack door. Its message was clear: "Get up, boys!
Wash up!" — or at least "Get dressed!" Twenty minutes later
the second gong said, "Breakfast's on and the cookhouse
door is open."

All meals were hefty. Hard work and fresh air gave us voracious
appetites which we were so busy satisfying that we hardly
talked. I found myself eating three times as much as I had
back home.

At breakfast the table was heaped with plates of flapjacks,
mountains of them, big bowls of porridge and tin dishes
of fried baloney, bacon, potatoes, beans and stacks of camp-
baked bread. Enamelware jugs held tea, coffee and milk;
the milk came from cans. I missed the natural milk I was
used to.

Each cookee was assigned a table and he hung around eyeing the
plates in case any needed a refill. We were charged only
$1.25 a day then for room and board, but if you weren't working
for some reason, even that could seem quite expensive. If
you slept late, or didn't get back from work on time, you went
hungry until the next meal.

4. Making Lunch

After breakfast there were usually two immediate chores. One was making lunch if your strip was too far off for you to walk back for the noonday meal. Many of the ingredients were leftovers from the breakfast table made into sandwiches. Does anyone know how delicious cold baked beans are in a sandwich? After cake and pie were packed into the lunchbox, we filled in the corners with hard-boiled eggs. Often they cracked when the cover was forced shut but, round or flat, they still tasted good.

5. The Outhouse

The camp sewage and waterworks were the most basic for there wasn't any point in installing water pipes. Once the forest within walking distance of the camp had been cut, the camp was abandoned and a new one built further out. The other chore, particularly to those like myself eager to be off making money, was sitting on the hole of an outdoor privy. (Back home I had liked the robust earthy smell of outhouses, with the bluebottle flies hanging around the door and singing in the sunshine.) Some lumberjack privies were many-holed — as many as six in a row — so there would be no waiting. On the strip, of course, if one got the urge, it was done by squatting nature style and using leaves for toilet paper.

6. "Driving"

"Driving" at that time meant floating pulpwood downriver to
Lake Superior. There the logs were corralled by tugboat
into a big boom and towed further along the shore to the pulp
mill. Some of us students were placed at the river's
source to push, or roll, the 4-foot pieces into the water. Others
were stationed at regular intervals or in special trouble
spots along the stream to watch for logs stopping or jamming
together. When this happened, they had to be freed
quickly before a major jam developed.

The drive tool was a long, slender pole with a metal hook-and-
point head on it. If the river was high, I could sit down
at the job, build a shelter against the frequent rains and heat
up water for tea in a tin can. (There was very little fire
hazard so early in the year.) But if the river was low, I had to
hustle to keep the wood moving. Sometimes I even had
to call for help from the student stationed next to me along the
bank.

The biggest and most admired man in the camp — properly so —
was the foreman, Pete Rodvick, a Lithuanian. He never
wasted a movement and he hardly ever spoke. But one day,
after watching me working on the stretch of the Little Pic
River that I patrolled, he addressed me in Ukrainian. I was so
thrilled at this unusual friendly gesture, I worked all the
harder.

There were days, I remember, when the rain began as a drizzle
in the morning and gradually increased until it came
down in torrents. If Pete judged it would go on for the rest of
the day, he called off the drive and we all trudged back to
camp in squishing wet boots feeling like drowned rats.

7. Dynamiting a Log Jam

Every log was valuable. The average 4-foot log was worth about
sixteen cents then and produced about 26 square feet of
newsprint for the Canadian and U.S. markets.

The previous year the Little Pic River had been so high that a
large mass of logs had been trapped in trees above sharp
bends in the stream. The company decided that it would pay to
put those of us students who had stuck out the rough life
till mid-June onto the job of skidding the trapped timber into the
water. "Big George," the Ukrainian, was in charge, and
we students worked our way further down the Little Pic than
we had ever been until we were stopped by rapids.

There was an enormous log jam stretched right across the river.
None of our poles could budge it. There was only one thing
to try. A charge of dynamite was submerged in the jam at what
appeared to Big George to be the nodal point. It was wired
to a detonator a safe distance away. Pete knelt down out of
harm's way, while George pushed the plunger.

WHAM! WHOOSH! A large column of water, smoke, logs
and splinters of logs burst into the air. But the jam stayed
put. And so did the column of water and logs — forever in my
memory — to come out later in sketches and finally in this
painting as a memorial to a bush operation now considered waste-
ful and out-of-date.

8. Notching

I never did match the old-timers in skill, and I doubt if I ever could have. I didn't have the patience to keep my tools in good working condition, and I had to work all the harder to compensate.

The first thing a good lumberjack does is decide which way he wants a tree to fall. That's the side he cuts a notch on. A properly sharpened axe does it in a few seconds with two or three short swings. The notch should be just slightly lower than where the saw cut will be made on the opposite side of the trunk. I never figured out the physics of it, I just did as I was told!

9. Felling

If the tree stood on what was to be the strip road, the tree had to be cut off right at ground level. This is so sleds hauling the cords in winter wouldn't get hung up on the stump or overturn because of it. If it was not on the actual road, the stump could be left a few inches higher, and that made it easier to saw.

In this painting I show how a tree is cut off close to the ground. To reach that low position with the swede saw, so that the arms hold the saw easily and the blade runs horizontally without twisting, a man has to wrap himself around the tree. It looks strange and awkward. But it's really the best way, once you're used to it.

In a northern camp, no one worked without a shirt on, even when it was hot. It wasn't just the insects. One's body was pressed against rough twigs and bark nearly all day, not only when cutting a tree but also when clearing the strip. A heavy shirt was a necessary protection.

10. Clearing the Strip Road

The strip boss or foreman marked off the strip boundaries with
eye-level axe blazes on the tree trunks. The strips ran parallel
to each other and were usually 22 yards wide, so that they could
accommodate the length of a tree felled toward the center.
That was the place you wanted the tree to fall to cut down as
much as possible on the work of carrying the wood you
had bucked, or sawed, to the cord pile. Once the tree had been
felled, limbed and bucked, the leftovers had to be thrown,
pushed or lifted off the strip road.

Any terrain was fine for a strip as long as it was reasonably
level. What really mattered to the lumberjack was how
rich the forest floor was. If it was poor land, then the forest
floor was scrubby, which meant extra work clearing the
strip road. Also, the trees were further apart, so you had to
carry your logs further and the trees had more and
thicker branches, which meant extra axe work limbing the tree.

The lumberjack hoped for good land. Then there were many
more trees growing closer together, which gave you
several advantages. The trees vied with each other for sunshine
and air, so they shot straight up for the sun. They grew
tall and didn't waste energy putting out branches on their lower
half, which meant next to no limbing. Also, their fight for
living room at the top meant they effectively cut off most of the
sunshine on the forest floor, making it impossible for
shrubs to grow. The forest floor instead was covered with a
carpet of pine needles, ideal for walking on and
cutting over.

11. Building a Cord Cradle

When the lumberjack judged he had enough logs for a cord,
or several cords, he set about building a cord cradle.
A cord is 4 feet high, 4 feet wide, and 8 feet long. Thin or
useless logs were used to make a framework to hold
that quantity of wood alongside the strip road. I made this
lithograph to show how it was done. Two upright poles
were stuck into the ground at either end and braced against an
under-frame. A notched crossbar held the vertical poles
together at the top. The logs were then piled in. The saw was
used as a rough measure because it was approximately
4 feet long, from tip to tip.

12. Piling a Cord

A poor cradle sometimes fell apart and then had to be rebuilt.
My worst problem with cradles occurred when I was
cutting white poplar. I did this at the Estonian camp only, for
I happened to be there the week or two that the sap was
running — that's when poplar is cut because the peeling is easier.

The poplars that grow in evergreen forests are healthy giants
compared to the scrawny punks we know on the prairies.
(They have to grow that big to rise above the spruce for sunshine
and air.) They average a foot in diameter and fill a cord
very quickly. But I'm afraid the time I gained in the cutting was
lost in the piling. Fresh-skinned poplar logs are slippery
as fish. Just when you think you have the pile made, before
your incredulous eyes the whole thing suddenly slides
apart in every direction, leaving a jumble of logs on the ground.
Then you have to start over.

And even after the cord seems to be holding, it's still treacherous.
You can come to your strip in the morning to find that a cord
or two has slipped apart during the night.

13. After the Sauna

There was an hour or two of glorious nudity every few days for
the lumberjack in camps influenced by Finnish culture.
That was sauna time. In a special shack or log cabin usually
built near a lake, a big pile of stones was heaped on a
box stove set into the floor. A fire was built in the stove and
stoked to red hot intensity. Several barrels of water were
placed in the room which was dimly lit by a single little window.
When the stones were hot enough, buckets of water were
dumped over them to raise clouds of steam.

A bank of benches rising on one side of the room, much like
a chicken roost, provided different intensity of heat and
steam. The higher the bench the hotter the atmosphere. When
it got too hot, you moved to a lower one. Only the
toughest and most experienced sauna enthusiast could occupy
the top bench. After sweating out the dirt and ashes of
several days from our pores and muscles, we would pour buckets
of cold water over our heads. Or, stark naked, we'd
rush out the door, racing the mosquitoes down to the boat
dock, and plunge into the lake.

Those northern lakes never really warmed up more than two or
three feet below the surface. Beneath that they seemed
permanently ice cold. The shock of sinking below that perma-
frost level was exhilarating — after you emerged.

14. Finnish Sour Drink

In the Estonian camp, several barrels of Finnish *kalijaa* stood at the back of the cook shack. This is a sour drink made of water, molasses, raisins, lemons and yeast that is consumed before it has fermented and therefore has no alcoholic content.

The advantages of *kalijaa* over water was that it quenched thirst quicker and didn't give the headachy, weak feeling one got from drinking a gallon of water at one go — something one could easily do, having worked up a great thirst.

On the strip itself water could often be found in deep little pools at the foot of trees standing in muskeg swamps. But you had to examine it carefully before drinking. If it was warm, it usually had mosquito larvae in it and if it tasted soapy, it had potash in it from the tree stumps.

15. Washing Up

The bull cook hauled water from the lake in barrels placed on a sled pulled by horses or a tractor. In winter he had to cut a hole in the ice. All day long pails, boilers or jugs of water sat on the camp stoves warming for cooking or washing. A pail with a dipper in it stood by the wash basins. In summer, cold water in this tin pail served for drinking or washing up after work.

Anyone wanting to shave had to heat his own water or get it from the cook shack. Some of the men washed, stripped to the waist. I did, too, until one of the former Nazis in the camp began counting my ribs and teasing me for being so skinny.

16. Sharpening the Saw

A foreman once told me, "A tidy work area and properly sharpened tools are half the job done already." It's true that a well-sharpened saw blade meant more wood cut with less effort. But "sharpening" was one of my failures. That's why it was such a pleasure for me to buy a new blade. It worked beautifully for some time with no need for sharpening or setting. But I couldn't do that very often because the expense hurt.

The two tools used for saw maintenance are a diamond file and a tooth setter. A swede saw blade has one raker for each four teeth; it pushes out the sawdust that the teeth make. These rakers have to be touched up with a file, too. Sharpening and setting are done on one's knee, or — as in this painting — in a nitch cut in the top of a tall stump. It was often an evening chore, done after supper. The most preferred spot was out in the middle of a clearing. There the wind might blow the mosquitoes away, and one could take full advantage of the remaining evening sunlight.

17. Axe Grinding

Axe grinding was a less frequent chore. I was told that a really sharp axe was less dangerous than a dull one. A dull one was likely to glance off the tree into your leg. But I refused to believe that; I hated tool sharpening so much. My troubles were also due to sleepiness, the result of the intense work schedule I was on. I got careless and broke axe handles.

Two kinds of axe handles were sold by the company: birch and oak. Birch was cheaper, so I chose it, but one false move and a branch could catch the handle just below the axe head and snap it off, like ice. Oak, on the other hand, was so tough it would often break the branch. Even when the handle itself broke, it could be taped up and used. Smart lumberjacks stowed away a spare handle and extra saw blades on their strips so that they would not waste time walking back to camp for new ones.

18. Laundry

Every man had to do his own laundry. It was a chore that was avoided as long as possible. Usually it was done on Sunday. If clothes got wet in the rain or snow they were hung around the box stove on wires or cords to dry. Bushmen went in for bright colors, usually big checks. Perhaps because they were colorful individuals. Or perhaps so they could see one another and avoid felling a tree on a campmate.

In winter, if a lumberjack took a mackinaw to his strip, he'd take it off once he got working because of the heat his body generated. He wore several pairs of socks in winter, one pair in summer, and they smelled because he perspired so much. His boots often had rubber bottoms for he walked in muskeg moss which was frequently saturated with water. Good old leather soles were even better because leather breathed, but it meant an extra evening chore of oiling or dubbining. A lumberman's pants just covered the tops of his boots.

19. Cook in the Kitchen

Here the cook chopped up beef while his cookee peeled potatoes. Sometimes those who found the work in the bush too tough took on the job of cook's helper rather than go back home immediately. They still had the pride of wearing lumberjack clothes, but they had to wear an apron over them. Their work was like punishment in the army; they had to do all the tedious, dirty jobs the cook didn't want to do. Also they had to get up earlier and go to bed later than the lumberjacks; at mealtime they served as waiters; afterward, they washed the dishes — which were usually enamelware to cut breakage.

20. Relaxation

Except for the dining room in the cook's shack, the bunkhouse
was the only other locale for social or recreational life.
There the lumberjack would stretch out, boots and all, on the
coarse gray blanket on his bed. He exchanged stories
with the occupants of the beds on either side.

If someone could play a mouth organ or accordion he was
much appreciated. I remember one old Finn with a
wooden radio that could receive only one station. Sputtering
with static one evening, it still gave me my most memorable
cultural experience of camp life, a reading of T. S. Eliot's
Murder in the Cathedral.

I was so starved for art and music that I ordered a hand-wound
record player by mail, and was able to crank out very
uneven renditions of "The Blue Danube," "La Donna e
Mobile" and of Galli-Curci singing Shakespeare's
"Lo, Hear the Gentle Lark."

The other men played cards or talked. Tony, a Polish lumberjack, could speak some Ukrainian, so he chose a bed
next to mine to have someone to communicate with. The
wall against his bed was plastered with pinups and
magazines and, even more than the other lumberjacks, he
loved to describe his experiences with women.

The lumberman's philosophy was supposed to be work hard,
save up, then go to town (usually a frontier city like
Fort William or Port Arthur) and, in a few days or weeks,
let the women and taverns clean out your pockets.
Afterward, with a devil-may-care attitude, you retired to the
woods to make another stake. That certainly was Tony.
But my sheltered upbringing made his stories embarrassing to me.

Most of the other lumberjacks at the camp at that particular
time were new immigrants, who had come to Canada after
World War II. They, like myself, were earning stakes; and they
meant to invest theirs in families, homes or small
businesses once they came out of the woods.

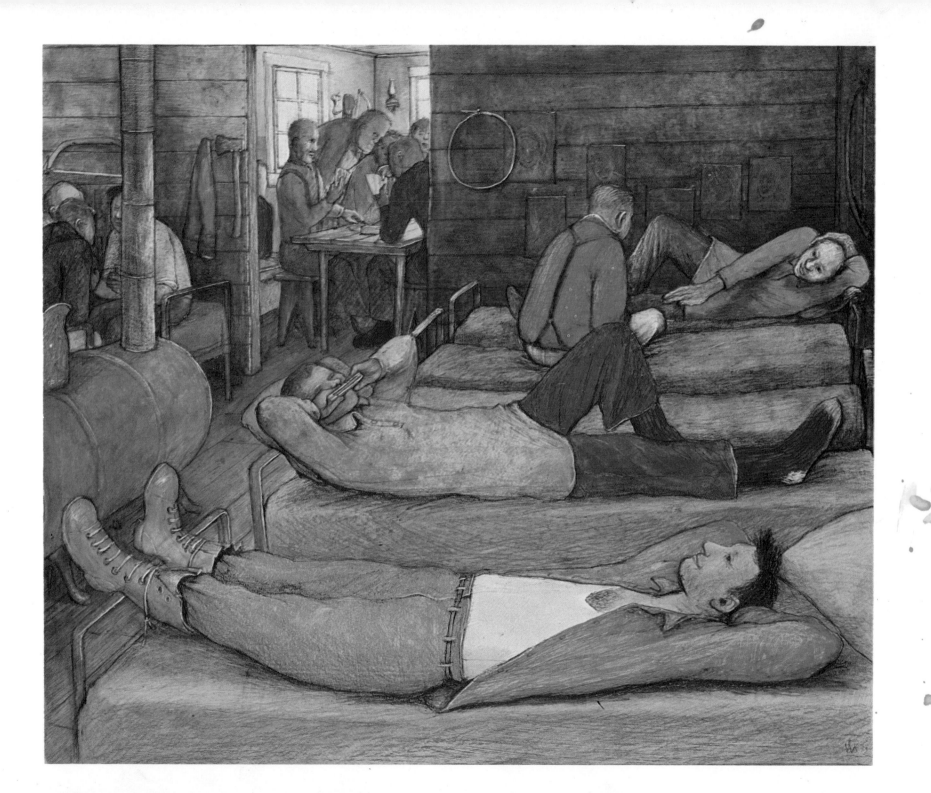

21. Working in the Rain

None of the other men, however pressing their ambition,
seemed as fanatic as I about making a stake. I was the
only one in our camp who worked nonstop throughout
those days when the rain came down. The others gave
up and went in to play cards. I found that by wearing a fisher-
man's complete black rubber outfit, I could keep on
working. I perspired a lot, but I didn't get wet from the
outside.

It was rather scary being left out there by myself in the
gloomy forest with dark, heavy clouds hovering over the
treetops. During some storms jagged bolts of lightning came
only a split second before tremendous crashes of thunder
showing how close I was to danger. Later on, in winter snow-
storms, I also seemed to be alone out there. Just big
Mother Nature and little me, fiddling around at her feet. I
remember thinking on such occasions how lucky I was
not to be hit by anything so that my father could say: "See, I
told you!"

I often remembered my father's gloomy predictions. The
closest any came to fulfillment was once when I cut
a tree that was leaning at an angle against another. It snapped
off before I could dodge it: the butt whirled around and
landed on the side of my foot, pinning it to the ground.
Luckily, the ground was pillow-soft muskeg moss, so I
managed to wiggle out from under. After checking for broken
bones, I went right on cutting. My goal was two and
a half cords, or $17.00 a day, every day, Sunday included.
That meant working twelve hours a day come hell or
high water.

22. The Lost Tree

It was winter that ended my bush days. The cold didn't
particularly bother me and since the days were shorter,
I got more rest. But the deep snow exhausted me. I found
it hard enough just to wade around in it up to my knees.
Handling logs in it as well was just too difficult. I developed a
pain in my chest from heavy breathing.

After a heavy snowfall, it was disheartening to see a tree I
had just felled disappear from sight in the snow,
leaving only an outline on the surface. Perhaps here and
there a branch might protrude to thumb its nose at me.
I might have struggled on another month or so. But there was
no need to, really. I had reached the savings figure of
$2000.00 that I had set before leaving the city. That was a
sizable stake back in 1951.

23. Hauling Pulpwood

There was only one operation I missed by leaving that month,
the pulpwood hauling, and I have had to depend on the
descriptions of other people for the information in this painting.
Horses and tractors were used, and the wood was hauled
on sleds from the cord piles right onto the river ice. With the
spring breakup, the logs would start their own way
downstream.

An iron hook shaped like a sharpened question mark, with
an elliptical handle, was a great help in lifting logs off
the cord pile and flinging them onto the sled. With one hand
you dug the sharpened point of it into one end of the
log, while the other end was cradled in your other arm near
the wrist. Using it well gave a good boost to the morale
because it required skill not to jab the hook into your leg.

The sled could be loaded with a single pile of logs as it is in
this picture. Or on a somewhat wider sled, there could be
double rows sloping inward toward the center to give greater
stability. Whenever the riverbank was steep, sled shoe
brakes were applied. The horses also helped to hold back
the load as the drivers reined them in. Occasionally
an unskilled driver saw his load overturn, but he learned to be
more careful next time since he was paid only for the
cords he got down onto the ice.

24. Return to Camp in Winter

The early setting of the sun in winter forced me to return with
the others in good time for supper at the camp. As the sun
dropped behind the trees, an icy winter chill closed around us. It
was a raw cold, with a raw sunset-colored sky.

As I walked, my swede saw was draped across my chest and
shoulder like an army rifle, the sharpened edge of the
blade facing backward. This left my hands free for the axe and
the lunch kit. The snowbound trail was just wide
enough for walking single file, so if you were joined by other
cutters along the way, you conversed over your
shoulder while your breath came out as steaming wraiths.

The darkness of the forest closing in behind seemed to be
driving us back to the tiny nucleus of human habitation
that was our camp.

25. The Bunkhouse — After Midnight

All of the men turned in early. Certainly you never saw anyone
up past midnight. In winter the bunkhouse took on a ghostly
séance look after the lights were put out.

Here and there in the dark a body stirred involuntarily; here
and there were snorers, or someone mumbling in his
sleep. The only light danced forth in rosy blotches from the
stove grill onto the floor. Occasionally it flared enough
to reveal socks drying on a pile of firewood.

Since the wood was usually poplar or birch, it gave a pleasant
smell. The colder it got the more the wood was heaped
on — the bull cook's chore — until the drum sides of the
stove glowed red from the heat. The windows were frosted
over with a half-inch of artwork by a better artist than I—
He who gave me such talent as I have.

Epilogue: The Harvester

In the twenty-three years since my two Estonian companions
and I trudged out of the woods for the last time, there has
been a revolution in the trade of the lumberjack.

Huge mechanical marvels called tree harvesters have arrived.
They resemble giant insects from another planet, and
they are driven by bushmen wearing hard hats and sitting in
air-conditioned cabs. They move relentlessly over all
obstacles as they methodically snip trees off at the ground,
strip them, cut them up and pile the logs into their
racks. When these are filled, the machines move out to dis-
charge their green gold onto huge trailer-trucks. Neither
night nor rain nor snow can stop them.

Ironically, it was my own brother John — the one who had
shared all those winters and summers with me and my
sister Winnie on the prairies — who led the team of engineers
that devised and perfected the tree harvester. John had
always been the mechanically clever one in the family.

The harvester can cut forty cords of wood in eight hours and
haul it out as well. The most I could cut in twelve hours
was two-and-a-half cords. But modern timber companies also
replant forests that have been cut out. I'm afraid we left
Nature to handle our ravages as best she could.

Was our old way, for all its hardships, more romantic, more
humane, more socially satisfying? I leave the answers
to others. I only know I am glad to have been a part of that
good life before it passed into history.